This crochet journal belongs to:

Dedication

This crochet log book is perfect for anyone who loves to crochet and make something that they can be proud of. Crocheting is a favorite hobby of many and this book is to make your next crochet project the best it can be. Enjoy!

How to use this crochet journal

This ultimate *Crochet Project notebook* is a perfect way to track and record all your crocheting activities. This unique review log book is a great way to keep all of your important information all in one place.

Each interior page includes prompts and space to record the following:

Project Number - Write which number project you are working on.
Project Name - Record the project name.
Created For - Write what person you are making this for.
Start Date - Keep track of your projects by entering the date it was started.
End Date - Record the date completed.
Hook - Stay on task by entering the crochet hook size.
Pattern - Use this box to label which pattern is being made, hat, headband, blanket...etc.
Design Source - Record your inspiration, simple shapes, stitches used.
Gauge - Write out the number of stitches per inch and rows per inch...so as to be reminded later..
Extra Tools - Keep track of measuring tape, rulers, stitch markers, scissors and so forth..
Yarn Type - Stay on task by labeling the yarn color, brand, dye lot, and Skeins.
Yarn Sample/Label - Attach a yarn sample, or label here.
Sketch/Photo - Blank Space to draw out a sketch or attach a photo of the current project.

If you are new to crocheting or have been at it for a while, this *Crochet Project Journal* is a must have! Can make an awesome gift for craft and crochet hobby lovers!

Enjoy!

PROJECT #		HOOK
PROJECT NAME		PATTERN
CREATED FOR		DESIGN SOURCE
START DATE		GAUGE
END DATE		EXTRA TOOLS

YARN TYPE

COLOR(S)	BRAND	DYE LOT #	SKEINS

YARN SAMPLE / LABEL

ATTACH YARN SAMPLE / LABEL HERE

SKETCH / PHOTO

🖼️ PROJECT #	✏️ HOOK
🧢 PROJECT NAME	🪡 PATTERN
🎁 CREATED FOR	✂️ DESIGN SOURCE
⏱️ START DATE	📏 GAUGE
🚩 END DATE	🧶 EXTRA TOOLS

YARN TYPE

✧ COLOR(S)	🏷️ BRAND	||||| DYELOT #	🧶 SKEINS

YARN SAMPLE / LABEL

ATTACH YARN SAMPLE / LABEL HERE

SKETCH / PHOTO

PROJECT #		HOOK	
PROJECT NAME		PATTERN	
CREATED FOR		DESIGN SOURCE	
START DATE		GAUGE	
END DATE		EXTRA TOOLS	

YARN TYPE

COLOR(S)	BRAND	DYE LOT #	SKEINS

YARN SAMPLE / LABEL

ATTACH YARN SAMPLE / LABEL HERE

SKETCH / PHOTO

PROJECT #	HOOK
PROJECT NAME	PATTERN
CREATED FOR	DESIGN SOURCE
START DATE	GAUGE
END DATE	EXTRA TOOLS

YARN TYPE

COLOR(S)	BRAND	DYE LOT #	SKEINS

YARN SAMPLE / LABEL

ATTACH YARN SAMPLE / LABEL HERE

SKETCH / PHOTO

PROJECT #	
PROJECT NAME	
CREATED FOR	
START DATE	
END DATE	

HOOK	
PATTERN	
DESIGN SOURCE	
GAUGE	
EXTRA TOOLS	

YARN TYPE

COLOR(S)	BRAND	DYE LOT #	SKEINS

YARN SAMPLE / LABEL

ATTACH YARN SAMPLE / LABEL HERE

SKETCH / PHOTO

PROJECT #		HOOK	
PROJECT NAME		PATTERN	
CREATED FOR		DESIGN SOURCE	
START DATE		GAUGE	
END DATE		EXTRA TOOLS	

YARN TYPE

COLOR(S)	BRAND	DYE LOT #	SKEINS

YARN SAMPLE / LABEL

ATTACH YARN SAMPLE / LABEL HERE

SKETCH / PHOTO

PROJECT #		HOOK	
PROJECT NAME		PATTERN	
CREATED FOR		DESIGN SOURCE	
START DATE		GAUGE	
END DATE		EXTRA TOOLS	

YARN TYPE

COLOR(S)	BRAND	DYE LOT #	SKEINS

YARN SAMPLE / LABEL

ATTACH YARN SAMPLE / LABEL HERE

SKETCH / PHOTO

- PROJECT #
- PROJECT NAME
- CREATED FOR
- START DATE
- END DATE

- HOOK
- PATTERN
- DESIGN SOURCE
- GAUGE
- EXTRA TOOLS

YARN TYPE

✦ COLOR(S)	BRAND	DYE LOT #	SKEINS

YARN SAMPLE / LABEL

ATTACH YARN SAMPLE / LABEL HERE

SKETCH / PHOTO

PROJECT #	
PROJECT NAME	
CREATED FOR	
START DATE	
END DATE	

HOOK	
PATTERN	
DESIGN SOURCE	
GAUGE	
EXTRA TOOLS	

YARN TYPE

COLOR(S)	BRAND	DYE LOT #	SKEINS

YARN SAMPLE / LABEL

ATTACH YARN SAMPLE / LABEL HERE

SKETCH / PHOTO

PROJECT #	HOOK
PROJECT NAME	PATTERN
CREATED FOR	DESIGN SOURCE
START DATE	GAUGE
END DATE	EXTRA TOOLS

YARN TYPE

COLOR(S)	BRAND	DYE LOT #	SKEINS

YARN SAMPLE / LABEL

ATTACH YARN SAMPLE / LABEL HERE

SKETCH / PHOTO

PROJECT #		HOOK	
PROJECT NAME		PATTERN	
CREATED FOR		DESIGN SOURCE	
START DATE		GAUGE	
END DATE		EXTRA TOOLS	

YARN TYPE

COLOR(S)	BRAND	DYE LOT #	SKEINS

YARN SAMPLE / LABEL

ATTACH YARN SAMPLE / LABEL HERE

SKETCH / PHOTO

- PROJECT #
- PROJECT NAME
- CREATED FOR
- START DATE
- END DATE

- HOOK
- PATTERN
- DESIGN SOURCE
- GAUGE
- EXTRA TOOLS

YARN TYPE

COLOR(S)	BRAND	DYE LOT #	SKEINS

YARN SAMPLE / LABEL

ATTACH YARN SAMPLE / LABEL HERE

SKETCH / PHOTO

PROJECT #		HOOK
PROJECT NAME		PATTERN
CREATED FOR		DESIGN SOURCE
START DATE		GAUGE
END DATE		EXTRA TOOLS

YARN TYPE

COLOR(S)	BRAND	DYE LOT #	SKEINS

YARN SAMPLE / LABEL

ATTACH YARN SAMPLE / LABEL HERE

SKETCH / PHOTO

PROJECT #	HOOK
PROJECT NAME	PATTERN
CREATED FOR	DESIGN SOURCE
START DATE	GAUGE
END DATE	EXTRA TOOLS

YARN TYPE

COLOR(S)	BRAND	DYE LOT #	SKEINS

YARN SAMPLE / LABEL

ATTACH YARN SAMPLE / LABEL HERE

SKETCH / PHOTO

PROJECT #	HOOK
PROJECT NAME	PATTERN
CREATED FOR	DESIGN SOURCE
START DATE	GAUGE
END DATE	EXTRA TOOLS

YARN TYPE

COLOR(S)	BRAND	DYE LOT #	SKEINS

YARN SAMPLE / LABEL

ATTACH YARN SAMPLE / LABEL HERE

SKETCH / PHOTO

PROJECT #	HOOK
PROJECT NAME	PATTERN
CREATED FOR	DESIGN SOURCE
START DATE	GAUGE
END DATE	EXTRA TOOLS

YARN TYPE

COLOR(S)	BRAND	DYE LOT #	SKEINS

YARN SAMPLE / LABEL

ATTACH YARN SAMPLE / LABEL HERE

SKETCH / PHOTO

PROJECT #	HOOK
PROJECT NAME	PATTERN
CREATED FOR	DESIGN SOURCE
START DATE	GAUGE
END DATE	EXTRA TOOLS

YARN TYPE

COLOR(S)	BRAND	DYE LOT #	SKEINS

YARN SAMPLE / LABEL

ATTACH YARN SAMPLE / LABEL HERE

SKETCH / PHOTO

- PROJECT #
- PROJECT NAME
- CREATED FOR
- START DATE
- END DATE

- HOOK
- PATTERN
- DESIGN SOURCE
- GAUGE
- EXTRA TOOLS

YARN TYPE

COLOR(S)	BRAND	DYE LOT #	SKEINS

YARN SAMPLE / LABEL

ATTACH YARN SAMPLE / LABEL HERE

SKETCH / PHOTO

PROJECT #		HOOK
PROJECT NAME		PATTERN
CREATED FOR		DESIGN SOURCE
START DATE		GAUGE
END DATE		EXTRA TOOLS

YARN TYPE

COLOR(S)	BRAND	DYE LOT #	SKEINS

YARN SAMPLE / LABEL

ATTACH YARN SAMPLE / LABEL HERE

SKETCH / PHOTO

PROJECT #	HOOK
PROJECT NAME	PATTERN
CREATED FOR	DESIGN SOURCE
START DATE	GAUGE
END DATE	EXTRA TOOLS

YARN TYPE

COLOR(S)	BRAND	DYE LOT #	SKEINS

YARN SAMPLE / LABEL

ATTACH YARN SAMPLE / LABEL HERE

SKETCH / PHOTO

PROJECT #	HOOK
PROJECT NAME	PATTERN
CREATED FOR	DESIGN SOURCE
START DATE	GAUGE
END DATE	EXTRA TOOLS

YARN TYPE

COLOR(S)	BRAND	DYE LOT #	SKEINS

YARN SAMPLE / LABEL

ATTACH YARN SAMPLE / LABEL HERE

SKETCH / PHOTO

PROJECT #	HOOK
PROJECT NAME	PATTERN
CREATED FOR	DESIGN SOURCE
START DATE	GAUGE
END DATE	EXTRA TOOLS

YARN TYPE

COLOR(S)	BRAND	DYE LOT #	SKEINS

YARN SAMPLE / LABEL

ATTACH YARN SAMPLE / LABEL HERE

SKETCH / PHOTO

PROJECT #		HOOK	
PROJECT NAME		PATTERN	
CREATED FOR		DESIGN SOURCE	
START DATE		GAUGE	
END DATE		EXTRA TOOLS	

YARN TYPE

COLOR(S)	BRAND	DYE LOT #	SKEINS

YARN SAMPLE / LABEL

ATTACH YARN SAMPLE / LABEL HERE

SKETCH / PHOTO

PROJECT #	HOOK
PROJECT NAME	PATTERN
CREATED FOR	DESIGN SOURCE
START DATE	GAUGE
END DATE	EXTRA TOOLS

YARN TYPE

COLOR(S)	BRAND	DYE LOT #	SKEINS

YARN SAMPLE / LABEL

ATTACH YARN SAMPLE / LABEL HERE

SKETCH / PHOTO

PROJECT #		HOOK
PROJECT NAME		**PATTERN**
CREATED FOR		**DESIGN SOURCE**
START DATE		**GAUGE**
END DATE		**EXTRA TOOLS**

YARN TYPE

COLOR(S)	BRAND	DYE LOT #	SKEINS

YARN SAMPLE / LABEL

ATTACH YARN SAMPLE / LABEL HERE

SKETCH / PHOTO

- PROJECT #
- PROJECT NAME
- CREATED FOR
- START DATE
- END DATE

- HOOK
- PATTERN
- DESIGN SOURCE
- GAUGE
- EXTRA TOOLS

YARN TYPE

COLOR(S)	BRAND	DYE LOT #	SKEINS

YARN SAMPLE / LABEL

ATTACH YARN SAMPLE / LABEL HERE

SKETCH / PHOTO

	PROJECT #		HOOK
	PROJECT NAME		PATTERN
	CREATED FOR		DESIGN SOURCE
	START DATE		GAUGE
	END DATE		EXTRA TOOLS

YARN TYPE

COLOR(S)	BRAND	DYE LOT #	SKEINS

YARN SAMPLE / LABEL

ATTACH YARN SAMPLE / LABEL HERE

SKETCH / PHOTO

PROJECT #	HOOK
PROJECT NAME	PATTERN
CREATED FOR	DESIGN SOURCE
START DATE	GAUGE
END DATE	EXTRA TOOLS

YARN TYPE

COLOR(S)	BRAND	DYE LOT #	SKEINS

YARN SAMPLE / LABEL

ATTACH YARN SAMPLE / LABEL HERE

SKETCH / PHOTO

PROJECT #	**HOOK**
PROJECT NAME	**PATTERN**
CREATED FOR	**DESIGN SOURCE**
START DATE	**GAUGE**
END DATE	**EXTRA TOOLS**

YARN TYPE

COLOR(S)	BRAND	DYE LOT #	SKEINS

YARN SAMPLE / LABEL

ATTACH YARN SAMPLE / LABEL HERE

SKETCH / PHOTO

- PROJECT #
- PROJECT NAME
- CREATED FOR
- START DATE
- END DATE
- HOOK
- PATTERN
- DESIGN SOURCE
- GAUGE
- EXTRA TOOLS

YARN TYPE

COLOR(S)	BRAND	DYE LOT #	SKEINS

YARN SAMPLE / LABEL

ATTACH YARN SAMPLE / LABEL HERE

SKETCH / PHOTO

PROJECT #		HOOK	
PROJECT NAME		PATTERN	
CREATED FOR		DESIGN SOURCE	
START DATE		GAUGE	
END DATE		EXTRA TOOLS	

YARN TYPE

COLOR(S)	BRAND	DYE LOT #	SKEINS

YARN SAMPLE / LABEL

ATTACH YARN SAMPLE / LABEL HERE

SKETCH / PHOTO

- PROJECT #
- PROJECT NAME
- CREATED FOR
- START DATE
- END DATE

- HOOK
- PATTERN
- DESIGN SOURCE
- GAUGE
- EXTRA TOOLS

YARN TYPE

COLOR(S)	BRAND	DYE LOT #	SKEINS

YARN SAMPLE / LABEL

ATTACH YARN SAMPLE / LABEL HERE

SKETCH / PHOTO

PROJECT #	HOOK
PROJECT NAME	PATTERN
CREATED FOR	DESIGN SOURCE
START DATE	GAUGE
END DATE	EXTRA TOOLS

YARN TYPE

COLOR(S)	BRAND	DYE LOT #	SKEINS

YARN SAMPLE / LABEL

ATTACH YARN SAMPLE / LABEL HERE

SKETCH / PHOTO

PROJECT #		HOOK	
PROJECT NAME		PATTERN	
CREATED FOR		DESIGN SOURCE	
START DATE		GAUGE	
END DATE		EXTRA TOOLS	

YARN TYPE

COLOR(S)	BRAND	DYE LOT #	SKEINS

YARN SAMPLE / LABEL

ATTACH YARN SAMPLE / LABEL HERE

SKETCH / PHOTO

	PROJECT #
	PROJECT NAME
	CREATED FOR
	START DATE
	END DATE

	HOOK
	PATTERN
	DESIGN SOURCE
	GAUGE
	EXTRA TOOLS

YARN TYPE

COLOR(S)	BRAND	DYE LOT #	SKEINS

YARN SAMPLE / LABEL

ATTACH YARN SAMPLE / LABEL HERE

SKETCH / PHOTO

PROJECT #	
PROJECT NAME	
CREATED FOR	
START DATE	
END DATE	

HOOK	
PATTERN	
DESIGN SOURCE	
GAUGE	
EXTRA TOOLS	

YARN TYPE

COLOR(S)	BRAND	DYE LOT #	SKEINS

YARN SAMPLE / LABEL

ATTACH YARN SAMPLE / LABEL HERE

SKETCH / PHOTO

PROJECT #	HOOK
PROJECT NAME	PATTERN
CREATED FOR	DESIGN SOURCE
START DATE	GAUGE
END DATE	EXTRA TOOLS

YARN TYPE

COLOR(S)	BRAND	DYE LOT #	SKEINS

YARN SAMPLE / LABEL

ATTACH YARN SAMPLE / LABEL HERE

SKETCH / PHOTO

- PROJECT #
- PROJECT NAME
- CREATED FOR
- START DATE
- END DATE

- HOOK
- PATTERN
- DESIGN SOURCE
- GAUGE
- EXTRA TOOLS

YARN TYPE

COLOR(S)	BRAND	DYE LOT #	SKEINS

YARN SAMPLE / LABEL

ATTACH YARN SAMPLE / LABEL HERE

SKETCH / PHOTO

PROJECT #		HOOK	
PROJECT NAME		PATTERN	
CREATED FOR		DESIGN SOURCE	
START DATE		GAUGE	
END DATE		EXTRA TOOLS	

YARN TYPE

COLOR(S)	BRAND	DYE LOT #	SKEINS

YARN SAMPLE / LABEL

ATTACH YARN SAMPLE / LABEL HERE

SKETCH / PHOTO

- PROJECT #
- PROJECT NAME
- CREATED FOR
- START DATE
- END DATE

- HOOK
- PATTERN
- DESIGN SOURCE
- GAUGE
- EXTRA TOOLS

YARN TYPE

COLOR(S)	BRAND	DYE LOT #	SKEINS

YARN SAMPLE / LABEL

ATTACH YARN SAMPLE / LABEL HERE

SKETCH / PHOTO

	PROJECT #		HOOK
	PROJECT NAME		PATTERN
	CREATED FOR		DESIGN SOURCE
	START DATE		GAUGE
	END DATE		EXTRA TOOLS

YARN TYPE

COLOR(S)	BRAND	DYE LOT #	SKEINS

YARN SAMPLE / LABEL

ATTACH YARN SAMPLE / LABEL HERE

SKETCH / PHOTO

PROJECT #	HOOK
PROJECT NAME	PATTERN
CREATED FOR	DESIGN SOURCE
START DATE	GAUGE
END DATE	EXTRA TOOLS

YARN TYPE

COLOR(S)	BRAND	DYE LOT #	SKEINS

YARN SAMPLE / LABEL

ATTACH YARN SAMPLE / LABEL HERE

SKETCH / PHOTO

PROJECT #		HOOK
PROJECT NAME		PATTERN
CREATED FOR		DESIGN SOURCE
START DATE		GAUGE
END DATE		EXTRA TOOLS

YARN TYPE

COLOR(S)	BRAND	DYE LOT #	SKEINS

YARN SAMPLE / LABEL

ATTACH YARN SAMPLE / LABEL HERE

SKETCH / PHOTO

- PROJECT #
- PROJECT NAME
- CREATED FOR
- START DATE
- END DATE

- HOOK
- PATTERN
- DESIGN SOURCE
- GAUGE
- EXTRA TOOLS

YARN TYPE

COLOR(S)	BRAND	DYE LOT #	SKEINS

YARN SAMPLE / LABEL

ATTACH YARN SAMPLE / LABEL HERE

SKETCH / PHOTO

PROJECT #		HOOK
PROJECT NAME		PATTERN
CREATED FOR		DESIGN SOURCE
START DATE		GAUGE
END DATE		EXTRA TOOLS

YARN TYPE

COLOR(S)	BRAND	DYE LOT #	SKEINS

YARN SAMPLE / LABEL

ATTACH YARN SAMPLE / LABEL HERE

SKETCH / PHOTO

PROJECT #	HOOK
PROJECT NAME	PATTERN
CREATED FOR	DESIGN SOURCE
START DATE	GAUGE
END DATE	EXTRA TOOLS

YARN TYPE

COLOR(S)	BRAND	DYE LOT #	SKEINS

YARN SAMPLE / LABEL

ATTACH YARN SAMPLE / LABEL HERE

SKETCH / PHOTO

PROJECT #	
PROJECT NAME	
CREATED FOR	
START DATE	
END DATE	

HOOK	
PATTERN	
DESIGN SOURCE	
GAUGE	
EXTRA TOOLS	

YARN TYPE

COLOR(S)	BRAND	DYE LOT #	SKEINS

YARN SAMPLE / LABEL

[ATTACH YARN SAMPLE / LABEL HERE]

SKETCH / PHOTO

	PROJECT #		HOOK
	PROJECT NAME		PATTERN
	CREATED FOR		DESIGN SOURCE
	START DATE		GAUGE
	END DATE		EXTRA TOOLS

YARN TYPE

COLOR(S)	BRAND	DYE LOT #	SKEINS

YARN SAMPLE / LABEL

ATTACH YARN SAMPLE / LABEL HERE

SKETCH / PHOTO

PROJECT #		HOOK
PROJECT NAME		**PATTERN**
CREATED FOR		**DESIGN SOURCE**
START DATE		**GAUGE**
END DATE		**EXTRA TOOLS**

YARN TYPE

COLOR(S)	BRAND	DYE LOT #	SKEINS

YARN SAMPLE / LABEL

ATTACH YARN SAMPLE / LABEL HERE

SKETCH / PHOTO

PROJECT #	HOOK
PROJECT NAME	PATTERN
CREATED FOR	DESIGN SOURCE
START DATE	GAUGE
END DATE	EXTRA TOOLS

YARN TYPE

COLOR(S)	BRAND	DYE LOT #	SKEINS

YARN SAMPLE / LABEL

ATTACH YARN SAMPLE / LABEL HERE

SKETCH / PHOTO

- PROJECT #
- PROJECT NAME
- CREATED FOR
- START DATE
- END DATE
- HOOK
- PATTERN
- DESIGN SOURCE
- GAUGE
- EXTRA TOOLS

YARN TYPE

COLOR(S)	BRAND	DYE LOT #	SKEINS

YARN SAMPLE / LABEL

ATTACH YARN SAMPLE / LABEL HERE

SKETCH / PHOTO

PROJECT #	HOOK
PROJECT NAME	PATTERN
CREATED FOR	DESIGN SOURCE
START DATE	GAUGE
END DATE	EXTRA TOOLS

YARN TYPE

COLOR(S)	BRAND	DYE LOT #	SKEINS

YARN SAMPLE / LABEL

ATTACH YARN SAMPLE / LABEL HERE

SKETCH / PHOTO

PROJECT #			HOOK	
PROJECT NAME			PATTERN	
CREATED FOR			DESIGN SOURCE	
START DATE			GAUGE	
END DATE			EXTRA TOOLS	

YARN TYPE

COLOR(S)	BRAND	DYE LOT #	SKEINS

YARN SAMPLE / LABEL

ATTACH YARN SAMPLE / LABEL HERE

SKETCH / PHOTO

PROJECT #	HOOK
PROJECT NAME	PATTERN
CREATED FOR	DESIGN SOURCE
START DATE	GAUGE
END DATE	EXTRA TOOLS

YARN TYPE

COLOR(S)	BRAND	DYE LOT #	SKEINS

YARN SAMPLE / LABEL

ATTACH YARN SAMPLE / LABEL HERE

SKETCH / PHOTO

	PROJECT #
	PROJECT NAME
	CREATED FOR
	START DATE
	END DATE

	HOOK
	PATTERN
	DESIGN SOURCE
	GAUGE
	EXTRA TOOLS

YARN TYPE

COLOR(S)	BRAND	DYE LOT #	SKEINS

YARN SAMPLE / LABEL

ATTACH YARN SAMPLE / LABEL HERE

SKETCH / PHOTO

- PROJECT #
- PROJECT NAME
- CREATED FOR
- START DATE
- END DATE

- HOOK
- PATTERN
- DESIGN SOURCE
- GAUGE
- EXTRA TOOLS

YARN TYPE

COLOR(S)	BRAND	DYE LOT #	SKEINS

YARN SAMPLE / LABEL

ATTACH YARN SAMPLE / LABEL HERE

SKETCH / PHOTO

- PROJECT #
- PROJECT NAME
- CREATED FOR
- START DATE
- END DATE

- HOOK
- PATTERN
- DESIGN SOURCE
- GAUGE
- EXTRA TOOLS

YARN TYPE

COLOR(S)	BRAND	DYE LOT #	SKEINS

YARN SAMPLE / LABEL

ATTACH YARN SAMPLE / LABEL HERE

SKETCH / PHOTO

PROJECT #	HOOK
PROJECT NAME	PATTERN
CREATED FOR	DESIGN SOURCE
START DATE	GAUGE
END DATE	EXTRA TOOLS

YARN TYPE

COLOR(S)	BRAND	DYE LOT #	SKEINS

YARN SAMPLE / LABEL

ATTACH YARN SAMPLE / LABEL HERE

SKETCH / PHOTO

PROJECT #	HOOK
PROJECT NAME	PATTERN
CREATED FOR	DESIGN SOURCE
START DATE	GAUGE
END DATE	EXTRA TOOLS

YARN TYPE

COLOR(S)	BRAND	DYE LOT #	SKEINS

YARN SAMPLE / LABEL

ATTACH YARN SAMPLE / LABEL HERE

SKETCH / PHOTO

PROJECT #	
PROJECT NAME	
CREATED FOR	
START DATE	
END DATE	

HOOK	
PATTERN	
DESIGN SOURCE	
GAUGE	
EXTRA TOOLS	

YARN TYPE

COLOR(S)	BRAND	DYE LOT #	SKEINS

YARN SAMPLE / LABEL

ATTACH YARN SAMPLE / LABEL HERE

SKETCH / PHOTO

	PROJECT #		HOOK
	PROJECT NAME		PATTERN
	CREATED FOR		DESIGN SOURCE
	START DATE		GAUGE
	END DATE		EXTRA TOOLS

YARN TYPE

COLOR(S)	BRAND	DYE LOT #	SKEINS

YARN SAMPLE / LABEL

ATTACH YARN SAMPLE / LABEL HERE

SKETCH / PHOTO

PROJECT #	HOOK
PROJECT NAME	PATTERN
CREATED FOR	DESIGN SOURCE
START DATE	GAUGE
END DATE	EXTRA TOOLS

YARN TYPE

COLOR(S)	BRAND	DYE LOT #	SKEINS

YARN SAMPLE / LABEL

ATTACH YARN SAMPLE / LABEL HERE

SKETCH / PHOTO

PROJECT #	HOOK
PROJECT NAME	PATTERN
CREATED FOR	DESIGN SOURCE
START DATE	GAUGE
END DATE	EXTRA TOOLS

YARN TYPE

COLOR(S)	BRAND	DYE LOT #	SKEINS

YARN SAMPLE / LABEL

ATTACH YARN SAMPLE / LABEL HERE

SKETCH / PHOTO

PROJECT #		HOOK
PROJECT NAME		PATTERN
CREATED FOR		DESIGN SOURCE
START DATE		GAUGE
END DATE		EXTRA TOOLS

YARN TYPE

COLOR(S)	BRAND	DYE LOT #	SKEINS

YARN SAMPLE / LABEL

ATTACH YARN SAMPLE / LABEL HERE

SKETCH / PHOTO

PROJECT #		HOOK	
PROJECT NAME		PATTERN	
CREATED FOR		DESIGN SOURCE	
START DATE		GAUGE	
END DATE		EXTRA TOOLS	

YARN TYPE

COLOR(S)	BRAND	DYE LOT #	SKEINS

YARN SAMPLE / LABEL

ATTACH YARN SAMPLE / LABEL HERE

SKETCH / PHOTO

PROJECT #	HOOK
PROJECT NAME	PATTERN
CREATED FOR	DESIGN SOURCE
START DATE	GAUGE
END DATE	EXTRA TOOLS

YARN TYPE

COLOR(S)	BRAND	DYE LOT #	SKEINS

YARN SAMPLE / LABEL

ATTACH YARN SAMPLE / LABEL HERE

SKETCH / PHOTO

🖼 PROJECT #	✏️ HOOK
🧶 PROJECT NAME	🧶 PATTERN
🎁 CREATED FOR	📐 DESIGN SOURCE
⏱ START DATE	📏 GAUGE
🚩 END DATE	🧵 EXTRA TOOLS

YARN TYPE

✦ COLOR(S)	🏷 BRAND	||||| DYE LOT #	🧶 SKEINS

YARN SAMPLE / LABEL

ATTACH YARN SAMPLE / LABEL HERE

SKETCH / PHOTO

PROJECT #	
PROJECT NAME	
CREATED FOR	
START DATE	
END DATE	

HOOK	
PATTERN	
DESIGN SOURCE	
GAUGE	
EXTRA TOOLS	

YARN TYPE

COLOR(S)	BRAND	DYE LOT #	SKEINS

YARN SAMPLE / LABEL

ATTACH YARN SAMPLE / LABEL HERE

SKETCH / PHOTO

PROJECT #		HOOK	
PROJECT NAME		PATTERN	
CREATED FOR		DESIGN SOURCE	
START DATE		GAUGE	
END DATE		EXTRA TOOLS	

YARN TYPE

✦ COLOR(S)	🏷 BRAND	||||| DYE LOT #	🧶 SKEINS

YARN SAMPLE / LABEL

ATTACH YARN SAMPLE / LABEL HERE

SKETCH / PHOTO

	PROJECT #
	PROJECT NAME
	CREATED FOR
	START DATE
	END DATE

	HOOK
	PATTERN
	DESIGN SOURCE
	GAUGE
	EXTRA TOOLS

YARN TYPE

COLOR(S)	BRAND	DYE LOT #	SKEINS

YARN SAMPLE / LABEL

ATTACH YARN SAMPLE / LABEL HERE

SKETCH / PHOTO

PROJECT #	HOOK
PROJECT NAME	PATTERN
CREATED FOR	DESIGN SOURCE
START DATE	GAUGE
END DATE	EXTRA TOOLS

YARN TYPE

COLOR(S)	BRAND	DYE LOT #	SKEINS

YARN SAMPLE / LABEL

ATTACH YARN SAMPLE / LABEL HERE

SKETCH / PHOTO

PROJECT #		HOOK
PROJECT NAME		PATTERN
CREATED FOR		DESIGN SOURCE
START DATE		GAUGE
END DATE		EXTRA TOOLS

YARN TYPE

COLOR(S)	BRAND	DYE LOT #	SKEINS

YARN SAMPLE / LABEL

ATTACH YARN SAMPLE / LABEL HERE

SKETCH / PHOTO

PROJECT #		HOOK	
PROJECT NAME		PATTERN	
CREATED FOR		DESIGN SOURCE	
START DATE		GAUGE	
END DATE		EXTRA TOOLS	

YARN TYPE

COLOR(S)	BRAND	DYE LOT #	SKEINS

YARN SAMPLE / LABEL

ATTACH YARN SAMPLE / LABEL HERE

SKETCH / PHOTO

PROJECT #		HOOK	
PROJECT NAME		PATTERN	
CREATED FOR		DESIGN SOURCE	
START DATE		GAUGE	
END DATE		EXTRA TOOLS	

YARN TYPE

COLOR(S)	BRAND	DYE LOT #	SKEINS

YARN SAMPLE / LABEL

ATTACH YARN SAMPLE / LABEL HERE

SKETCH / PHOTO

PROJECT #	HOOK
PROJECT NAME	PATTERN
CREATED FOR	DESIGN SOURCE
START DATE	GAUGE
END DATE	EXTRA TOOLS

YARN TYPE

COLOR(S)	BRAND	DYE LOT #	SKEINS

YARN SAMPLE / LABEL

ATTACH YARN SAMPLE / LABEL HERE

SKETCH / PHOTO

	PROJECT #		HOOK
	PROJECT NAME		PATTERN
	CREATED FOR		DESIGN SOURCE
	START DATE		GAUGE
	END DATE		EXTRA TOOLS

YARN TYPE

COLOR(S)	BRAND	DYE LOT #	SKEINS

YARN SAMPLE / LABEL

ATTACH YARN SAMPLE / LABEL HERE

SKETCH / PHOTO

PROJECT #	HOOK
PROJECT NAME	PATTERN
CREATED FOR	DESIGN SOURCE
START DATE	GAUGE
END DATE	EXTRA TOOLS

YARN TYPE

COLOR(S)	BRAND	DYE LOT #	SKEINS

YARN SAMPLE / LABEL

ATTACH YARN SAMPLE / LABEL HERE

SKETCH / PHOTO

	PROJECT #			HOOK
	PROJECT NAME			PATTERN
	CREATED FOR			DESIGN SOURCE
	START DATE			GAUGE
	END DATE			EXTRA TOOLS

YARN TYPE

COLOR(S)	BRAND	DYE LOT #	SKEINS

YARN SAMPLE / LABEL

ATTACH YARN SAMPLE / LABEL HERE

SKETCH / PHOTO

🖼️ PROJECT #	✏️ HOOK
🧢 PROJECT NAME	🧶 PATTERN
🎁 CREATED FOR	✂️ DESIGN SOURCE
⏱️ START DATE	📏 GAUGE
🚩 END DATE	🧵 EXTRA TOOLS

YARN TYPE

✦ COLOR(S)	🏷️ BRAND	||||| DYE LOT #	🧶 SKEINS

YARN SAMPLE / LABEL

ATTACH YARN SAMPLE / LABEL HERE

SKETCH / PHOTO

PROJECT #	HOOK
PROJECT NAME	PATTERN
CREATED FOR	DESIGN SOURCE
START DATE	GAUGE
END DATE	EXTRA TOOLS

YARN TYPE

COLOR(S)	BRAND	DYE LOT #	SKEINS

YARN SAMPLE / LABEL

ATTACH YARN SAMPLE / LABEL HERE

SKETCH / PHOTO

- PROJECT #
- PROJECT NAME
- CREATED FOR
- START DATE
- END DATE

- HOOK
- PATTERN
- DESIGN SOURCE
- GAUGE
- EXTRA TOOLS

YARN TYPE

COLOR(S)	BRAND	DYE LOT #	SKEINS

YARN SAMPLE / LABEL

ATTACH YARN SAMPLE / LABEL HERE

SKETCH / PHOTO

PROJECT #		HOOK	
PROJECT NAME		PATTERN	
CREATED FOR		DESIGN SOURCE	
START DATE		GAUGE	
END DATE		EXTRA TOOLS	

YARN TYPE

COLOR(S)	BRAND	DYE LOT #	SKEINS

YARN SAMPLE / LABEL

ATTACH YARN SAMPLE / LABEL HERE

SKETCH / PHOTO

PROJECT #	HOOK
PROJECT NAME	PATTERN
CREATED FOR	DESIGN SOURCE
START DATE	GAUGE
END DATE	EXTRA TOOLS

YARN TYPE

COLOR(S)	BRAND	DYE LOT #	SKEINS

YARN SAMPLE / LABEL

ATTACH YARN SAMPLE / LABEL HERE

SKETCH / PHOTO

PROJECT #	HOOK
PROJECT NAME	PATTERN
CREATED FOR	DESIGN SOURCE
START DATE	GAUGE
END DATE	EXTRA TOOLS

YARN TYPE

COLOR(S)	BRAND	DYE LOT #	SKEINS

YARN SAMPLE / LABEL

ATTACH YARN SAMPLE / LABEL HERE

SKETCH / PHOTO

PROJECT #	HOOK
PROJECT NAME	PATTERN
CREATED FOR	DESIGN SOURCE
START DATE	GAUGE
END DATE	EXTRA TOOLS

YARN TYPE

COLOR(S)	BRAND	DYE LOT #	SKEINS

YARN SAMPLE / LABEL

ATTACH YARN SAMPLE / LABEL HERE

SKETCH / PHOTO

PROJECT #	HOOK
PROJECT NAME	PATTERN
CREATED FOR	DESIGN SOURCE
START DATE	GAUGE
END DATE	EXTRA TOOLS

YARN TYPE

COLOR(S)	BRAND	DYE LOT #	SKEINS

YARN SAMPLE / LABEL

ATTACH YARN SAMPLE / LABEL HERE

SKETCH / PHOTO

PROJECT #	HOOK
PROJECT NAME	PATTERN
CREATED FOR	DESIGN SOURCE
START DATE	GAUGE
END DATE	EXTRA TOOLS

YARN TYPE

COLOR(S)	BRAND	DYE LOT #	SKEINS

YARN SAMPLE / LABEL

ATTACH YARN SAMPLE / LABEL HERE

SKETCH / PHOTO

PROJECT #		HOOK
PROJECT NAME		PATTERN
CREATED FOR		DESIGN SOURCE
START DATE		GAUGE
END DATE		EXTRA TOOLS

YARN TYPE

COLOR(S)	BRAND	DYE LOT #	SKEINS

YARN SAMPLE / LABEL

ATTACH YARN SAMPLE / LABEL HERE

SKETCH / PHOTO

- PROJECT #
- PROJECT NAME
- CREATED FOR
- START DATE
- END DATE

- HOOK
- PATTERN
- DESIGN SOURCE
- GAUGE
- EXTRA TOOLS

YARN TYPE

✦ COLOR(S)	BRAND	DYE LOT #	SKEINS

YARN SAMPLE / LABEL

ATTACH YARN SAMPLE / LABEL HERE

SKETCH / PHOTO

PROJECT #	HOOK
PROJECT NAME	PATTERN
CREATED FOR	DESIGN SOURCE
START DATE	GAUGE
END DATE	EXTRA TOOLS

YARN TYPE

COLOR(S)	BRAND	DYE LOT #	SKEINS

YARN SAMPLE / LABEL

ATTACH YARN SAMPLE / LABEL HERE

SKETCH / PHOTO

🖼️ PROJECT #	✏️ HOOK
🧶 PROJECT NAME	🧶 PATTERN
🎁 CREATED FOR	📐 DESIGN SOURCE
⏱️ START DATE	📏 GAUGE
🚩 END DATE	🧵 EXTRA TOOLS

YARN TYPE

✦ COLOR(S)	🏷️ BRAND	▓ DYE LOT #	🧶 SKEINS

YARN SAMPLE / LABEL

ATTACH YARN SAMPLE / LABEL HERE

SKETCH / PHOTO

PROJECT #	
PROJECT NAME	
CREATED FOR	
START DATE	
END DATE	

HOOK	
PATTERN	
DESIGN SOURCE	
GAUGE	
EXTRA TOOLS	

YARN TYPE

COLOR(S)	BRAND	DYE LOT #	SKEINS

YARN SAMPLE / LABEL

ATTACH YARN SAMPLE / LABEL HERE

SKETCH / PHOTO

PROJECT #	HOOK
PROJECT NAME	PATTERN
CREATED FOR	DESIGN SOURCE
START DATE	GAUGE
END DATE	EXTRA TOOLS

YARN TYPE

COLOR(S)	BRAND	DYE LOT #	SKEINS

YARN SAMPLE / LABEL

ATTACH YARN SAMPLE / LABEL HERE

SKETCH / PHOTO

PROJECT #	
PROJECT NAME	
CREATED FOR	
START DATE	
END DATE	

HOOK	
PATTERN	
DESIGN SOURCE	
GAUGE	
EXTRA TOOLS	

YARN TYPE

COLOR(S)	BRAND	DYE LOT #	SKEINS

YARN SAMPLE / LABEL

ATTACH YARN SAMPLE / LABEL HERE

SKETCH / PHOTO

PROJECT #	HOOK
PROJECT NAME	PATTERN
CREATED FOR	DESIGN SOURCE
START DATE	GAUGE
END DATE	EXTRA TOOLS

YARN TYPE

COLOR(S)	BRAND	DYE LOT #	SKEINS

YARN SAMPLE / LABEL

ATTACH YARN SAMPLE / LABEL HERE

SKETCH / PHOTO

PROJECT #		HOOK
PROJECT NAME		PATTERN
CREATED FOR		DESIGN SOURCE
START DATE		GAUGE
END DATE		EXTRA TOOLS

YARN TYPE

COLOR(S)	BRAND	DYE LOT #	SKEINS

YARN SAMPLE / LABEL

ATTACH YARN SAMPLE / LABEL HERE

SKETCH / PHOTO

🖼 PROJECT #	✎ HOOK
🧢 PROJECT NAME	🕸 PATTERN
🎁 CREATED FOR	✏️ DESIGN SOURCE
⏱ START DATE	📏 GAUGE
🚩 END DATE	🧵 EXTRA TOOLS

YARN TYPE

✧ COLOR(S)	🏷 BRAND	||||| DYE LOT #	🧶 SKEINS

YARN SAMPLE / LABEL

ATTACH YARN SAMPLE / LABEL HERE

SKETCH / PHOTO

PROJECT #		HOOK
PROJECT NAME		**PATTERN**
CREATED FOR		**DESIGN SOURCE**
START DATE		**GAUGE**
END DATE		**EXTRA TOOLS**

YARN TYPE

COLOR(S)	BRAND	DYE LOT #	SKEINS

YARN SAMPLE / LABEL

ATTACH YARN SAMPLE / LABEL HERE

SKETCH / PHOTO

- PROJECT #
- PROJECT NAME
- CREATED FOR
- START DATE
- END DATE
- HOOK
- PATTERN
- DESIGN SOURCE
- GAUGE
- EXTRA TOOLS

YARN TYPE

COLOR(S)	BRAND	DYE LOT #	SKEINS

YARN SAMPLE / LABEL

ATTACH YARN SAMPLE / LABEL HERE

SKETCH / PHOTO

PROJECT #		HOOK
PROJECT NAME		**PATTERN**
CREATED FOR		**DESIGN SOURCE**
START DATE		**GAUGE**
END DATE		**EXTRA TOOLS**

YARN TYPE

COLOR(S)	BRAND	DYE LOT #	SKEINS

YARN SAMPLE / LABEL

ATTACH YARN SAMPLE / LABEL HERE

SKETCH / PHOTO

PROJECT #		HOOK	
PROJECT NAME		PATTERN	
CREATED FOR		DESIGN SOURCE	
START DATE		GAUGE	
END DATE		EXTRA TOOLS	

YARN TYPE

COLOR(S)	BRAND	DYE LOT #	SKEINS

YARN SAMPLE / LABEL

ATTACH YARN SAMPLE / LABEL HERE

SKETCH / PHOTO

- PROJECT #
- PROJECT NAME
- CREATED FOR
- START DATE
- END DATE
- HOOK
- PATTERN
- DESIGN SOURCE
- GAUGE
- EXTRA TOOLS

YARN TYPE

COLOR(S)	BRAND	DYE LOT #	SKEINS

YARN SAMPLE / LABEL

ATTACH YARN SAMPLE / LABEL HERE

SKETCH / PHOTO

PROJECT #	HOOK
PROJECT NAME	PATTERN
CREATED FOR	DESIGN SOURCE
START DATE	GAUGE
END DATE	EXTRA TOOLS

YARN TYPE

COLOR(S)	BRAND	DYE LOT #	SKEINS

YARN SAMPLE / LABEL

ATTACH YARN SAMPLE / LABEL HERE

SKETCH / PHOTO

PROJECT #	HOOK
PROJECT NAME	PATTERN
CREATED FOR	DESIGN SOURCE
START DATE	GAUGE
END DATE	EXTRA TOOLS

YARN TYPE

COLOR(S)	BRAND	DYE LOT #	SKEINS

YARN SAMPLE / LABEL

ATTACH YARN SAMPLE / LABEL HERE

SKETCH / PHOTO

- PROJECT #
- PROJECT NAME
- CREATED FOR
- START DATE
- END DATE

- HOOK
- PATTERN
- DESIGN SOURCE
- GAUGE
- EXTRA TOOLS

YARN TYPE

COLOR(S)	BRAND	DYE LOT #	SKEINS

YARN SAMPLE / LABEL

ATTACH YARN SAMPLE / LABEL HERE

SKETCH / PHOTO

PROJECT #		HOOK	
PROJECT NAME		PATTERN	
CREATED FOR		DESIGN SOURCE	
START DATE		GAUGE	
END DATE		EXTRA TOOLS	

YARN TYPE

COLOR(S)	BRAND	DYE LOT #	SKEINS

YARN SAMPLE / LABEL

ATTACH YARN SAMPLE / LABEL HERE

SKETCH / PHOTO

www.ingramcontent.com/pod-product-compliance
Lightning Source LLC
Chambersburg PA
CBHW071402080526
44587CB00017B/3154